R · I · L · K · E
Between Roots

THE LOCKERT LIBRARY OF POETRY IN TRANSLATION

For other titles in the Lockert Library see page 61

For other titles in the Lockert Library see page 61

R·I·L·K·E
Between Roots

•

SELECTED POEMS RENDERED FROM THE

GERMAN BY RIKA LESSER WITH A NOTE

BY RICHARD HOWARD AND A PREFACE

BY RIKA LESSER   PRINCETON UNIVERSITY PRESS

Published by Princeton University Press, 41 William Street
Princeton, New Jersey 08540
In the United Kingdom: Princeton University Press, Guildford, Surrey

Library of Congress Cataloging in Publication Data will be
found on the last printed page of this book

ISBN 0-691-06668-X (cloth)
01429-9 (pbk.)

The Lockert Library of Poetry in Translation is supported by a bequest
from Charles Lacy Lockert (1888-1974)

This book has been composed in Linotron Electra
Clothbound editions of Princeton University Press books
are printed on acid-free paper, and binding materials are
chosen for strength and durability. Paperbacks, although satisfactory
for personal collections, are not usually suitable for library rebinding
Printed in the United States of America by Princeton University Press
Princeton, New Jersey

DESIGNED BY LAURY A. EGAN

"Ein Geliebtes: The Body of the Work" reprinted from *The Massachusetts Review*
Copyright 1975 The Massachusetts Review, Inc.

Some of these translations have appeared in slightly different form in
The American Poetry Review

For Judith Hoberman and Dominic Kinsley

Contents

A Preface: Ten Years Later xi

A Note on Rika Lesser's Rilke by Richard Howard xiii

ONE

Orpheus. Eurydice. Hermes 3

The Sonnets to Orpheus I, 5 6

The Sonnets to Orpheus I, 9 7

The Sonnets to Orpheus II, 15 8

Graves of the Hetaerae 9

Alcestis 11

Christ's Journey to Hell 14

Tears, tears that break out of me . . . 15

Odette R.... 16

Ô Lacrimosa 17

Lachrymatory 19

Give me, Earth, pure fired . . . 20

The Bowl of Roses 21

Inside the Rose 24

Today I want, for your sake, to feel . . . 25

Wild Rosebush 26

A Sequel to "The Bowl of Roses" 27

Arrival 28

Rose, pure Contradiction, Delight . . . 29

The Spanish Trilogy 30

Once I took your face between . . . 32

Looking up from the book, from the close, countable lines . . . 33

Night: into depth dissolved . . . 34

TWO

The Sonnets to Orpheus I, 2 37

The Sonnets to Orpheus I, 25 38

Requiem for a Friend   39

Requiem for Wolf Graf von Kalckreuth   47

Elegy   52

Antistrophes   54

The Sonnets to Orpheus II, 13   56

Pearls rolling away! Oh, did a string break . . . 57

The Sonnets to Orpheus II, 29   58

Come, you last thing I recognize . . .   59

A Preface: Ten Years Later

Holding Out, Poems rendered from the German of Rainer Maria Rilke by Rika Lesser, with *A Note* by Richard Howard, originally came out from Abattoir Editions in February 1976, having been printed by hand in an edition of two hundred and twenty-five copies during the spring and summer of the centennial of Rilke's birth, at the University of Nebraska at Omaha. The type face was Bembo with Romulus Open initials, the paper Grand Moghul hand made in India. The hand of the printer belonged to Harry Duncan. The book was beautiful and out of print by the end of the year.

Several years went by before, in February 1984—nearly ten years past the time I completed the original manuscript—I could come back to these renderings of Rilke and set about revising them. I am no longer, as Richard Howard calls me in his note, the "newest" translator of Rilke, but I still believe I am, if not *the* most, certainly among the most "faithful" of Rilke's English-language translators to date.

Coming back to the poems after so much time had passed gave me certain advantages and certain disadvantages. It had been more than ten years since I had read virtually all Rilke's writings and, under the tutelage of Professor Peter Demetz during my junior year at Yale, first began to translate Rilke's poetry in earnest. In my senior year, as a Scholar of the House, I had additional help in closely reading the German texts from Professor George C. Schoolfield, and constant advice about re-creating the poems in English from Richard Howard. A decade later the whole of Rilke's corpus was not exactly in the forefront of my brain; but in the interim, an indispensable tool for Rilke translators and scholars had appeared: a concordance to his poetry and plays. Going back to the German texts "afresh" in 1984, using the concordance to check on key words or instances of hapax legomenon, confirmed for me many connections I had made ten years earlier, brought them all back to mind.

But reading Rilke's poems again in German at thirty meant something quite different from reading them at twenty. Ten more years of "life" experience, ten years more of "literary" experience. Frankly, when I first sat down with *Holding Out* and the German texts again, I was terrified. Terrified that I might have changed too much in those years to re-enter and re-capture the spirit, linguistic and emotional, that went into the making of *Holding Out.* Terrified, too, that perhaps Rilke would not *mean* as much to me at thirty as he did at twenty.

I was both relieved and dismayed at what I found. He did mean as much—a tribute both to Rilke and to the nature of true love—but sometimes he *meant differently.* Here and there I came across lines or passages that I had translated in a way I could no longer understand, and I had to wrest my way through to a new comprehension of words, of lines, still very much open to interpretation. Perhaps my fate will be to come back to these again at forty and fifty. . . . Should any of you now reading this book have one of those two hundred and twenty-five copies of *Holding Out*, you will find that no new poems have been added nor any taken away, that the order of presentation has been preserved, and you will have to compare very hard, in some cases "down to each / dash that punctuates a pause—," to see what semantic adjustments have been made.

I owe enormous debts of gratitude to Peter Demetz, Richard Howard, and George Schoolfield for their assistance ten years ago, and more recently once again. But I owe another large debt to Harry Duncan, who, when I was one year old, published translations of eight poems of Rilke he had done himself (in *Poets of Today: Harry Duncan, Murray Noss, May Swenson,* New York: Scribner's, 1954). My own versions of seven of *The Sonnets to Orpheus,* thematically interspersed here, were conceived of and executed as prose exegeses. Reading page proofs in Sweden in 1975—at a time when nothing actually could be changed—I was furious with Harry for having lineated my prose versions to make them appear as sonnetlike as possible. He knew better than I did then, and in some cases now I have further relineated the sonnets—not to make them appear more proselike, but in order to make even better use of a resource of verse Harry Duncan chose to remind me of when he set the book in type.

Neither in the old nor in this new edition of Rilke's poems in English do the German texts appear. Nor are there notes beyond Rilke's own dedications. I continue to believe that those who can read the poems in German should and can do so and make of them what they will; translation is only a record of a reading. Those who do not know German are invited to compare these renderings with all the others available in English or other languages they may know, and to read the vast body of Rilke scholarship, a great deal of which I plunged into at and since the time I initially translated these poems. For none of us *is* Rilke, though many of us should have liked to be, if only in part.

RIKA LESSER

A Note on Rika Lesser's Rilke

In the parlor game of imaginary translations (Tennyson's *Aeneid*, Firbank's *Pillow-Book of Lady Sei Shonagon*, Hemingway's *Princess of Cleves*) there was one white hope that could not be darkened until 1973; Auden's *Rilke*. No other poet, not even Jarrell with his eighteen exuberant "adaptations," loomed so likely as the Auden who in 1939—in China!—thought of one

> *Who for ten years of drought and silence waited,*
> *Until in Muzot all his being spoke,*
> *And everything was given once for all.*
>
> *Awed, grateful, tired, content to die, completed,*
> *He went out in the winter night to stroke*
> *That tower as one pets an animal.*

But Auden did not translate Rilke. We are left with the myth—the Rilke who ransacked Europe from Russia to Ronda, from Karnak to Copenhagen, unable to release what was "given" save in fugitive explosions, igneous perceptions (as when he called Gide's translation of fragments from *Malte Laurids Brigge* "a labor equally that of Hercules and of Cinderella"). We are left, most of us, with the myth of Rilke without the poems. Here is a poet transcendentally "linguistic"—whose recuperation of Being depends more, I think, on verbal figures than any other maker's of our century—and yet we are so often left with no more than his "ideas," his concepts, those pale after-images. The rescued world of Rilke, from the very beginning, is explicitly designated, Paul de Man reminds us, as a world of words. And in English, we have not had the words, we do not yet read Rilke as a maker of verbal objects, but as a mystagogue, a prophet, a seer.

That is the great significance, for me, of what Rika Lesser has done here: she has translated *poems*. She has chosen certain works—they constitute a very particular vision of the poet, hard-edged one may say, and much less vaporous than what we had been vouchsafed before—which *can* be rendered, which can be realized on her own terms. What her terms are—the terms she has come to, I mean, with her own tongue—it is capital to know. I shall therefore quote here Rika Lesser's hostage to fortune, the poem which indicates her *posture* confronting the task:

Ein Geliebtes: The Body of the Work

FOR R.M.R.

1. Approach

Because you were not mine, I approached
you as I would any human being: hesitantly,
close-mouthed, from a distance. You seemed
both alive and dead, and I tried to work you
out from what others said about you.
Others who thought they knew you.
If I think back to our first meeting, our first
encounter, what impressed me most was your way
of walking: precise in every step.
There are, after all, walls between us.
And a background: but I too can see, "a round shard
with a red ground, upon which the taut legs
of a quadriga appear, like the black inscription
over an entrance."

So I returned your call, though at first
you were belligerent, even openly hostile to me:
Taunting me with puns, inventing words, or worse—
altering the old ones, with no respect for grammar.
Not trusting hearsay, I came to you myself
and held on tight until your Protean forms:
dead body of Christ, horses, butterflies,
eyelids of black-eyed roses, clear lachrymatories,
fruits, mirrors, angels, gods and God knows what,
turned and returned to one thing with no name,
something nameless and unspeakable. Like a magician
of the invisible, a clock without hands, you pointed to
things in you, in me, somewhere between: Images.
My curse on the words!

2. Depths

Like Christ's soul in Hell I plunged wilder
depths, heard cries howl toward me.
When the landscapes vanish, is it
my voice that speaks? Late at night,
in one ruinous flash, like an exhibitionist
you'll say, "I am your sleeper," and disappear.
Then like a painter faced with blanks, knowing
only no color is absolute, I reconstruct
from tone. Kinder than most, you utter
no loud demands, never look hurt, revenge
is not in your nature. But you just stand there,
clear as the Design in a cloudless sky at night,
and just as constant.

You've made your own defense, down to each
dash that punctuates a pause—, where
I hear music, see a rush of rain, feel a power
descending. But not to me; perhaps to me alone.
You delivered me from my chores to my work,
my real address. Some have too little faith.
We approximate in choosing. But are we lost?
We can only lose ourselves. And one good man
encouraged me to sustain our difficult rapport,
one flamboyant man
with the courage of all the French nation.

3. Vows

There are times I think our affair will never work out.
Bonds delude. Ceremonial diction rings false in
my voice. Praise cannot. Fruits rot, fall away:
but sometimes decay brings forth. The tree rises,
green ascends. How often have I had to turn to Root.
So dark down here, if I look up for an instant,
I'm sure to lose you. I must look down,

far down within myself, until I become
transparent, and your print, your imprint emerges.
No one can part us. Few can give advice.
You are my crutch, as long as I make you walk.
If there's a god in me, may it be the one of song.
May our words be flung into the invisible and there
live. If I turn wayward or willful,
give me your elegies.

It is humble, that posture, but not submissive; I believe she has the movement, the tone, the *intervals* which make room, as we say, for the poems, the seam between a talent and the soul. Her decision, for example, to jettison rhyme is a crucial one in the case of such a poet as Rilke—it is a decision to throw half the cargo overboard in order to bring the ship into port. The risks of her decision are ours, and Rika Lesser assumes them with enormous probity—the probity of a poet who knows how much must be given up, how much must be renounced, in order to "have" anything at all.

Proust, whose death coincided exactly with the completion of Rilke's work, suggests the attitude requisite, a willingness to give up verisimilitude for the sake of vision. The giving-up is all—in Rilke himself, whose surrender to joy, to pain, is perhaps unequalled in the history of poetic identity (Hölderlin . . . Keats . . . Leopardi: it is a tempting family tree, whose very roots are deciduous); and in this newest translator of his, a scholar of transparency rather than (mere) transport. The point, or the poignance, is to become "an ear of the earth," to let the earth—by which Rilke intends the dead as well as the living, the historical past as well as the ecstatic (because unknown) future—speak within us. Whereupon there will be no third persons, only address, only the transition from what was elegy to hymn, from lament to praise. Specific instances of this movement are the poems to Paula Modersohn-Becker and to Marina Tsvetaeva—instances, I mean, which become ecstasies by their hovering, wavering, undulant process, so that what was merely suspected and even suspect can be acclaimed and even claimed: the body *is* the soul, Rilke would have us know, in the most radical identification of spirit and matter since the Greeks. (Perhaps that is why Rika Lesser has put so many of Rilke's wonderful poems of the Greek world in her selection—they have, in their contours, within their firm outlines, a specific gravity no other culture can afford.)

I do not want to make claims for these new translations more tremendous than the pleasure they give, a pleasure bestowed by lucidity and love conjugated in that living twist of idiom we call style; but I think Rika Lesser deserves—if but for her relentless humility to meaning, in an endeavor where feeling *is* meaning—one tremendousness; let me say, then, that I am ready, with these poems in their English, to take on more than faith—faith being the substance of things hoped for, whereas here is the substance *given*—the claim that Rilke is not merely a great myth, not merely a great modernist, a great spiritual docent (Princess Marie's "Doktor Seraphicus") but, in the terrestrial sense, that sense of these words in this order, a great poet.

RICHARD HOWARD

O · N · E

Orpheus. Eurydice. Hermes

It was the souls' strange mine:
like silver ore they went, silent
as veins through its darkness. Between roots
sprang the blood that goes on to humans,
and heavy as porphyry it looked in the dark.
There was no other redness.

There were rocks
and spectral forests. Bridges over emptiness
and that great, gray, unreflecting pool
that hung over its distant bed
like rainclouds over a landscape.
And between meadows, soft and long-suffering,
showed the one pale path,
like a long strip of linen, bleaching.

And on this one path they came.

First, the slender man in the blue mantle,
who stared, mute and impatient, straight ahead.
In great bites his stride
devoured the path; his fists hung
heavy in the fall of folds
and forgot entirely the weightless lyre
that had grown into his left hand
like roses twining with the olive branch.
It was as if his senses were divided:
While sight ran before him like a dog,
turned back, again and again stood
distant and waiting at the path's next turn,—
hearing lagged behind him, like a scent.
Sometimes it seemed to him as if it reached
just to the movement of those other two,
who should be following this whole ascent.
Then again came only faint echoes of his climbing
and the wind in his mantle behind him.
He kept telling himself, they would still come;

said it aloud and heard his own words fade.
They would still come, only there would be two
who walked so terribly softly. Suppose he
turned just once (if only looking back
did not dissolve this whole task,
still incomplete), he had to see them,
the two soft ones who followed him in silence:

The god of journeys, of the distant message,
the petasos over his brilliant eyes,
bearing the slender staff before his body
and the wings beating at his ankles;
and given to his left hand: *she.*

So beloved
that from one lyre
more mourning came
than ever from threneteriai,
that a world grew out of mourning
in which everything existed all over again:
woods and a valley, and a path
and a village, field, stream, animals;
and around this world of mourning,
just as around the other earth,
a sun, and a silent, starry sky,
a mourning sky with stars displaced—:
So beloved.

But she walked on, at the god's hand,
her steps hobbled by the long shrouds,
uncertain, gentle, and without impatience.
Within herself
like a woman hopeful, heavy with child,
and thought not of the man who walked ahead,
nor of the path ascending into life.
Within herself. And having died
fulfilled her like an abundance.
Like a fruit of sweetness and of darkness,
she was so full of her great death,
which was so new, that she understood nothing.

She was again a virgin, again
untouchable; her sex, closed,
like a young flower toward evening,
and her hands were so broken
of being given, that even the gentle god's
infinitely soft and guiding touch
offended her, like a liberty taken.

Now she was no longer that blonde woman
sometimes remembered in the poet's songs,
no longer the broad bed's odor and island
and no longer that man's property.

She was already loosened like long hair
and scattered and absorbed like fallen rain
and meted out like hundredfold provision.

She was already root.

And when suddenly
the god restrained her,
and pronounced the doom: He has turned—,
she understood nothing and said softly: *Who?*

But distant, dark, before the bright opening
stood someone or other whose face
was not to be recognized. He stood and saw,
how on that strip of path between the meadows,
the god of message, silent, sorrowing, turned
to follow the shape
already going back that same way,
her steps hobbled by the long shrouds,
uncertain, gentle and without impatience.

The Sonnets to Orpheus I, 5

Erect no monument. Just let the rose
bloom each year for his sake. For it is
Orpheus: his metamorphosis in this one
and this. We should not trouble ourselves

with other names. Once and for all it is
Orpheus, whenever there's song. He comes
and goes. Isn't it much already, if sometimes
he survives the bowl of roses for a few days?

How he must vanish for you to comprehend,
even if he himself is anxious at vanishing!
While his word outstrips existence here,

he's already there, where you don't follow.
The lyre's lattice doesn't force his hands.
And he obeys, even as he transgresses.

The Sonnets to Orpheus I, 9

Only one who has already raised
the lyre, plucked its strings among
the shades as well, may surmising restore
the infinite praise.

Only one who has eaten of the poppy
with the dead, of their own
flower, will not lose even the most
imperceptible tone.

Even if the reflection in the pool
often swims before us, blurred:
Know the image.

Only in the Double Realm
will the voices become endless,
mild, liberal.

The Sonnets to Orpheus II, 15

O Fountain-Mouth, giving Mouth, not to be
drained, speaking one pure thing, incessantly,—
before the flowing face of the water, you,
mask of marble. And in the background

aqueducts, their descent. From afar, passing
tombs, from the slope of the Apennines, they
carry your Saying to you; then, on the black
aging, on your chin's decline, your Saying

is done, falls over into the basin standing
before you. This is the sleeping ear laid down,
the ear of marble into which you always speak.

An ear of the earth. Only to herself
does she speak this way. If a jug intrudes,
it seems to her you interrupt.

Graves of the Hetaerae

In their long hair they lie
with brown faces: they have retreated into themselves.
Eyes closed, as if before too great a distance.
Skeletons, mouths, and flowers. In the mouths
the polished teeth, like rows
of ivory pocket chessmen.
And flowers, yellow pearls, narrow bones,
hands and tunics, woven fabric wasting
over the heart that caved in. But there,
under those rings, those talismans
and gemstones like blue eyes (lovers' keepsakes),
the silent crypt of the sex abides,
filled to the fornix with petals.
And again yellow pearls, rolled apart,—
vessels of fired clay, whose contours
her own image once decorated, green shards
of oil jars smelling like flowers,
and tiny idols: household altars for
the rapturous gods in the heavens of hetaerae.
The broken cestus, flat scarabs,
small figures with colossal genitals,
laughing mouths, dancers, runners,
golden brooches: tiny bows as if for
hunting amulets of birds and animals,
long needles, household goods,
and a round shard with a red ground,
upon which the taut legs of a
quadriga appear, like the black
inscription over an entrance.
Again flowers, pearls that have rolled apart,
the bright loins of a tiny lyre,
and between veils that fall like mist,
as if it crawled out from the shoe's chrysalis:
the delicate butterfly of the ankle.

And so they lie, brimming with things,
precious things: gemstones, toys, housewares,

broken junk (what waste fell into them!)
and they darken, like the bed of a river.

They *were* riverbeds,
on the surface the bodies of many youths broke
in brief, quick waves
(that wanted to go further, to the next life)
and within them roared the torrents of men.
Sometimes boys broke out of the mountains
of childhood, dropped in tremulous cascades
and played with the things on the bottom,
until the slope stirred and seized their senses:

Then they filled the whole breadth of this broad
channel with clear, shallow water,
and set it swirling at the deep places;
and for the first time mirrored the banks
and the faint cries of birds—, while
the starry nights of a sweet country shot
into skies that nowhere would close.

Alcestis

Then suddenly the messenger was among them,
thrown into the fermenting wedding banquet
like brewer's yeast.
The drinkers did not notice the secret
entrance of the god, who hugged his godhood
to him like a wet cloak,
and seemed to be one of them, one or another
passing through. But suddenly, in the middle
of speaking, one of the guests saw
the young master at the head of the table,
somehow snatched up, no longer reclining,
and everywhere, his entire being mirroring
a strangeness that spoke terribly to him.
And then all at once, as if the mixture settled,
there was stillness; only, with the lees of muddy
din at the bottom, and a precipitate
of falling babble, already rotten, reeking
of musty laughter that had gone flat.
And then they recognized the slender god,
just as he was, inwardly full of mission
and inexorable,—they almost knew.
And yet, when it was uttered, it was
beyond all knowledge, not to be grasped at all.
Admetus must die. When? This very hour.

But he fractured the shell of his fear
and from the chips stuck out his hands
to bargain with the god:
for years, for one year more of youth,
for months, for weeks, for a few days,
O, not days, nights, only one,
One Night, just this one: for this.
The god denied him, and then he cried out,
outwards, let it all out, crying
as his mother cried out in childbirth.

And she came to him, an old woman,
and the father came as well, the old father,
and they both stood, old, lost, obsolete,
beside the crier who suddenly, as never before
so closely, saw them, stopped, gulped, and said:
Father,
does this mean much to you, what remains,
this scum that keeps you from swallowing?
Go, pour it off. And you, woman,
old Mother,
what more have you to do here: you have given birth.
And he held them both in one grip
like animals to be sacrificed. And then let them go,
pushed the old folks off, inspired, beaming,
drawing breath and calling: Creon! Creon!
And nothing but this; nothing but this name.
But in his face stood the Other,
waiting for the name he did not speak,
just as he proffered it to the young friend,
the beloved, glowingly across the bewildered table.
The old ones, obviously, are no ransom,
they are used up and wretched and nearly worthless,
but you, you, in your perfect beauty—

But then he no longer saw his friend,
who stayed behind, and what came forth was *she*,
even a little smaller than he knew her
and slight and sad in the pale wedding dress.
All the others are only her street,
down which she comes and comes—: (soon she will be
there in his arms that painfully unfold).

Still as he waits, she speaks; but not to him.
She speaks to the god, and the god hears her,
and now all hear it, as if within the god:

There can be no deputy. There is me.
I am deputy. For no one is at the end as I am.
What remains for me of what I was here?
What matters is my dying.

Did she not tell you, when she gave the order,
that the bed waiting in there
belongs to the underworld? I bade farewell.
Farewell after farewell.
None dying bids more. Oh yes, I went,
so that everything buried beneath Whatever
is now my husband may disperse and dissolve—;
so, lead me off: even now I die for him.

And like the wind on the high seas, veering,
the god strode, almost as to one dead,
and at once was distant from her husband,
to whom he tossed, implied in the gesture,
one hundred lives of earth.
He rushed, reeling toward the pair,
grasping for them as in dream. Already
they approached the entrance crowded
with red-eyed women. But once
more he saw the virgin's face, that turned
with a smile, bright as a hope,
almost a promise: to return grown,
from the deep death,
to him, the living one—

Then he flung
his hands before his face, just as he knelt there,
in order to see nothing more after that smile.

Christ's Journey to Hell

All suffered out, his being evaded the terrible
tormented body. Up there. Left it.
And the darkness, solitary, was afraid,
and at the pallor flung
bats:—even now in the evenings,
fear of colliding with that cold anguish
reels in their fluttering. Dark restless air
spent itself on the corpse: listlessness, torpor
in the strong wakeful animals of Night.
Released, his soul may have intended to belong
to the landscape, inactive. For his Passion's event
was enough. To him
the nighttime presence of things seemed measured,
and like a sorrowful space, from above, he embraced them.
But the earth, parched in the thirst of his wounds,
the earth burst open; cries came from its chasm.
He, agony's expert, heard Hell
howling toward him, craving awareness
of his pain's end: shocked in its continuing torture
to suspect, past the end of his endless, *its* end.
He plummeted downward, the soul, with exhaustion's
whole weight; hurriedly strode
through the startled backward look of pasturing shades,
glanced up at Adam, hastily,
hurried down, vanished, gleamed and was lost in plungings
of wilder depths. Suddenly (higher, higher) over the center
of seething cries, on the tall
tower of his endurance, he stepped forth: breathless,
stood, unprotected, possessor of pain. Kept silence.

Tears, tears that break out of me.
My death, Moor, bearer
of my heart, slant me, hold me
so they run off. I want to speak.

Black, gigantic heart-holder.
And if I spoke,
do you think the silence would break?

Cradle me, old friend.

Odette R....

Tears, the deepest ones, O *rise!*

When a life
has truly risen and from the clouds of its own stricken heart
falls back: we call that rain Death.

But all the more tangible becomes the dark to us, who are poor—,
all the more precious to us, who are rich, the strange kingdom of earth.

Ô Lacrimosa

(Trilogy for future music of Ernst Křenek)

I
Oh, the one full of tears, the withholding sky
grows heavy over the landscape of her pain.
And when she weeps, a gentle shower of rain
slants across, blows the sand-bed of the heart.

Oh heavy with tears. Scale to weigh all tears!
She did not consider herself sky, for she was clear,
and surely the sky exists only for the clouds.

How plain it grows, and how near, your Land of Pain,
beneath the one stern sky. Like a face
resting in its slow awakening,
Oh, to confront, to balance the depth of the world!

II
Nothing but a breath is Emptiness, and that
greenness of the lovely trees
in full leaf: a breath!
We, breathed upon still,
today still breathed upon, count
this slow breathing of the earth:
we are its haste.

III
But the winters! Oh this secret
pondering of the earth. There, round the dead
in the pure reversion of juices,
boldness gathers,
boldness of springs to come.
Where conceiving occurs
beneath rigor; where the threadbare

green of the great summers
grows again to new
insight and ruin, and to the mirror of foreboding;
where the flowers' color forgets
that lingering of our eyes.

The Bowl of Roses

Angry ones. You saw flickering, saw two angry
boys tangled into Something
that was hate, reeling along the ground
like an animal, fallen, attacked by bees;
performers, heaped up, towering overactors,
rampaging horses that collapsed,
casting sight away, teeth flashing,
as if the skull peeled off through the mouth.

But now you know how this is forgotten:
before you stands the bowl full of roses,
unforgettable, brimming with that
extreme of being and bending, offering,
never able to give, presence
that might be ours: our limit as well.

Life without sound, opening without end,
using space without taking space from that
space the objects all around diminish,
scarcely outlined, like a blank not yet painted,
and nothing but inwardness, strange and delicate
and self-illuminating—up to the rim:
Do we know anything at all like this?

And this: a feeling begins
because petals are touching petals?
And this: one opens like a lid,
and under it, nothing but eyelids,
closed ones, as if, in sleeping tenfold,
they had to subdue the power of inner sight.
And this above all: that through these petals
light must pass. Out of the thousand heavens
they slowly filter that drop of darkness,
in whose glare of fire the tousled bundle
of stamens is aroused and rises.

And the movement in the roses, look!
Gestures through such tiny angles of deflection,
they would remain invisible, if their rays
did not diverge and run into the universe.

See that white one that bloomed blissfully
and stands there in the big open petals
like a Venus, upright in the scallop shell;
and the blushing one, as if confused
turning to one of the cool ones,
and how the cool one withdraws, unresponsive,
and how the cold one stands, wrapt in itself,
among the open ones that doff everything.
And *what* they doff, light or heavy,
like a cloak, a load, a wing,
a mask, each according to its kind,
and *how* they doff it: as if before the beloved.

They can be— what? Wasn't that yellow one,
lying there hollow and open, the rind of a fruit,
in which the same yellowest juice was
more concentrated, almost orange?
And was it not already too much, this opening,
for this one, whose nameless pink took
in the air the bitter aftertaste of deep lilac?
And the cambric one, is it not a dress,
in which, still gentle and warm with breath,
the slip clings, both flung off
at the same time, before bathing
in the shadow of old cabins at dawn in the woods.
And this one here, opalescent porcelain,
fragile, a shallow China cup
brimming with tiny, bright butterflies,—
and that one, holding nothing but itself.

But aren't they all like that, holding only themselves,
when Continence means: the world out there,
wind, rain, patience of the spring,
debt, disquiet, veiled fate,

darkness of the earth at evening,
even the drift, flight and approach of clouds,
even the vague influence of distant stars:
to turn into a hand full of Inwardness.

Now all this lies heedless in the open roses.

Inside the Rose

Where for this Inside is there
an Outside? Upon what wound
does one lay such a dressing?
What heavens are reflected there
in the inland lake of these open roses,
these heedless ones, look:
How loose they lie, tempting fate,
as if no trembling hand
could ever spill them.
They can scarcely contain
themselves; many let themselves
be filled to the brim and over
flow with inner space
into days that always
fuller and fuller close,
until the whole summer becomes
a room, a room in a dream.

Today I want, for your sake, to feel
roses; to feel roses for your sake alone;
for your sake today I want for long, long
hours to feel roses unfelt, roses.

All bowls are filled; they lie
each in itself one hundredfold,
like valleys filled out by other valleys,
within themselves they lie, overburdened.

As unspeakable as the night
they overburden one who offers,
like stars above the plains
they overwhelm with pomp.
Rose-night, Rose-night.
Night of roses, night of many, many
bright roses, bright night of roses,
sleep of the rose-eyelids, the thousand,
bright rose-sleep, I am your sleeper:
Bright sleeper of your odors, deep
sleeper of your cool ardors.
As I, dwindling, give myself to you,
now you have my being to oppose.
May my fate dissolve into your
most incomprehensible Composure,
and the thrust of my unfolding
nowhere know an obstacle.
Rose-space, born within roses,
in roses secretly raised,
and from the open roses granted us
large as heart-space, that we may outside,
as well, feel within the Space of Roses.

Wild Rosebush

How it stands there before the darkenings
of the rainy evening, young and pure;
among its thrashed-out tendrils, giving,
and yet sunk, immersed in its rose-existence;

the shallow blossoms, some already open,
each one unasked-for and untended:
so, endlessly outdone by itself
and indescribably self-excited,

it calls to the wanderer, who in evening
meditation, passes by the path:
Oh see me stand, here, look, how safe I am
and unprotected, having all I need.

A Sequel to "The Bowl of Roses"

Written for Mme. Riccard

Rich was the room from them, fuller, fuller, more sated.
Roses, lingering ones: suddenly they are strewn.
In the evening perhaps. The determined fall of the petals
sounds, at the edge of the hearth, like faint applause.

Do they applaud Time, that has so tenderly slain them?
Did they themselves not endure long enough, escaping us too soon?
Look, the reddest ones are reddened out, almost black,
and every possible pallor has beset the paler ones.

Your Hereafter begins between pages of books;
irrepressible fragrance dwells in the chest, in the cupboard,
presses into a thing that serves us, winds into folded scarves
what seized us out of the roses, and what into roses sank.

Arrival

Inside a rose your bed stands, beloved. But you
(oh, I a swimmer against the stream of scent)
I have lost. Just as these thrice three months
(immeasurable from outside) are to life that's been lived,
so, once turned inward, shall I *be*. At once,
two millennia before that new being's creation
that we enjoy, when we begin to feel,
suddenly: facing you, I am born in the eye.

Rose, pure Contradiction, Delight,
to be No-one's Sleep under so many
Lids.

The Spanish Trilogy

[I]
Out of this cloud, look, the one that so savagely
covers the star that was just there—(and out of me),
out of this mountainous land beyond, that now
has night, for a time, the night winds—(and out of me),
out of this river at the bottom of the valley, capturing
the light of the ragged sky's clearing—(and out of me);
out of me and everything, Lord, to make
one single thing: out of me and the feeling
with which the herd, penned in the fold,
breathing, endures the great dark Nonexistence
of the world—, out of me and every light
in the dark Presence of the many houses, Lord:
to make one thing; out of the strangers, for
I know not one, Lord, and out of me, and me
to make *one* thing; out of the sleepers,
out of the strange old men in the asylum
who cough importantly in their beds, out of
children, drunk with sleep, at just as strange a breast,
out of much Tentativeness and always out of me,
out of nothing but me and what I do not know,
to make the thing, Lord, Lord, Lord, the thing,
at once of world and earth, like a meteor
that in its weight gathers only
the sum of flight:
weighing nothing but arrival.

[II]
Why is it that a man must go about and take to himself
strange things, as perhaps the porter who lifts
the strangely heavy and heavier shopping basket
from booth to booth, and laden, trails behind,
not daring to ask: Master, why this banquet?

Why is it that a man must stand there like a shepherd,
exposed to the excess of influence,
so much a part of this eventful space

that, leaning against a tree in the landscape, he
would have his Fate, without acting ever again.
And yet has not, in his far-too-large gaze,
the silent mitigation of the herd. Has
nothing but world, each time he raises his eyes,
each time he bows his head: world. What yields itself
gladly to others pierces him
inhospitably like music,
blindly enters his blood, changes and goes by.

There he gets up at night and already has
the outside cry of birds inside him
and feels bold, because he takes all
the stars into his face, heavily—, o not like the man
who prepares this night for his beloved
and spoils her with all the skies he's felt.

[III]
May I, when again I have the confusion
of cities, the tangled skein of uproar,
the throng of vehicles around me, may I, detached,
may I yet, beyond the agitation,
remember heaven and the brink of the mountains
the herd crossed, coming home.
May my courage be stony
and the daily task of the shepherd seem possible to me,
as he wanders, and weathers, and measuring his stone's throw,
drives in, mends the hem of his flock, where it frays.
Slow stride, not light, his body, ponderous,
all the same, his stance is glorious. A god still might
secretly enter this figure and be no less.
From time to time he lingers and moves along, like the day itself,
and the shadows of clouds pass through him,
as if Space slowly thought
thoughts for him.

Make of him what you will. As the wavering night-light
into the lamp's mantle, I place myself inside him.
A calmed light shines. Death, more
purely, would find its way.

Once I took your face between
my hands. Moonlight fell on it:
of all things the most incomprehensible
under overflowing tears.

Like something docile that endures in silence,
it was almost like an object one can hold.
And yet there was no creature in the cold
night, that endlessly evades me.

Look there—the places we stream toward,
pushing into the scant surface
all the waves of our heart,
pleasure, weakness,
and to whom do we finally offer them?

To the stranger, who misunderstood us,
to the other, whom we never found,
to the slave, who bound us,
to winds of spring, that vanished,
and to the silence, to Dame Loss.

Looking up from the book, from the close, countable lines,
into the fulfilled night outside:
O how like stars the packed feelings scatter,
as if a bunch of wild
flowers were untied:

Youth of lightness, and inclining sway of the heavy,
and the reluctant bend of the tender—.
Everywhere desire to restore and nowhere Demand;
surfeit of world, and earth enough.

Night: into depth dissolved,
your face upon my face.
You, my astonished sight's greatest
preponderance.

Night: in my glance trembling,
yet in yourself so firm;
inexhaustible creation, enduring
over residual earth;

full of young nebulas
whose rims in flight
throw fire into the soundless
adventure of the void:

by your mere being, O Transcendence,
how small I seem—;
yet, one with the dusky earth,
I dare, within you, to be.

$T \cdot W \cdot O$

The Sonnets to Orpheus I, 2

And almost a girl it was that came forth,
the joy of song and lyre made one. And through
her springtime veils she shone clearly.
And in my ear she made her own bed.

And in me she slept. Her sleep was everything: The trees,
how again and again I stood awestruck before them; this
distance that I can feel; the meadow that I know by feel;
and every astonishment that touched, that hurt my self.

She slept the world. You singing god, how did you make her
so perfect, so that at first she did not long to be awake?
See, she stands there, was always there, she rose, and slept.

Where is her death? How can you invent this theme before
your song consumes itself?—Even as she rises out of me,
she slips away, she sinks . . . A girl, almost . . .

The Sonnets to Orpheus I, 25

But it is now *you, you* whom I held as a flower, whose *name* was lost
to me; I no longer know it. In my lapse, I want to recall you *once* more,
to return you, to take you within me, so that I may show you to the others.
You have turned away from me; you are stolen from me; yet I know you
as a girl; I know you are the playmate of the cry that knows no conqueror.

At first she was a dancer. Dancing, she suddenly halted the body
that filled with hesitation. That hesitation fell into her while
her youngness (her youth spilled as molten ore) was cast in bronze.
Sorrowing and listening—. There and then, from the Capable Ones,
those High Powers, music fell to her, into her altered heart.

The sickness was near. Already the shadows entered the blood
with their dark powers; thickly, the blood pressed on. But
suddenly, like a fleeting suspicion, it broke forth
into its natural spring.

Again and again interrupted by darkness, by downfall;
again and again, earthly it shone. Until, after terrified
beating, it entered that open gate, that gate beyond which
no consolation is known.

(To Wera)

Requiem for a Friend

[In memoriam Paula Modersohn-Becker, 1876–1907]

I have Dead, and I let them go
and was amazed to see them so confident,
so soon at home in Being-dead, so right,
so unlike their reputation. Only you, you turn
back; you graze me, stalk, you want to knock
against something so that it sounds of you
and discloses you. O don't take from me what I am
slowly learning. I'm sure of this, you stray
when you are moved to nostalgia for
some thing or other. We transform things,
their presence is not here, perceived, we take
them in and reflect them from our Being.
  I thought you much farther away. It troubles me
that *you*, just you, should stray and come, you
who have worked more changes than any woman.
Not that we were frightened when you died,
nor that your strong death interrupted us
in darkness, tearing the Until-then from the Up-till-now:
this concerns us; to put them in order
will be our task, our common task.
But that you yourself were frightened and even now
are frightened, where fear no longer counts;
that you lose a shred of your Eternity
and enter here, Friend, here,
where all does not yet exist; that you,
for the first time dispersed and divided in Everything,
did not grasp the rising of the infinite forces
as here you grasped each thing;
that from the orbit which had already received you,
the mute gravity of restlessness
dragged you down to counted Time—:
this often wakes me at night, like a thief breaking in.
And if I may say that you only deign to come,
out of generosity, out of prodigality,

because you are so sure of yourself, so in your self,
that you go about like a child, not afraid
of the places where harm can come—:
but no: you beg. This cuts me
right to the bone like the sharp cry of a saw.
Like a reproach a ghost might make me,
a grudge you might bear against me when at night
I draw myself back into my lungs, into the pit of my body,
into the last, poorest chamber of my heart,—
such a reproach would not be so cruel
as this begging. What do you ask?

    Tell me— must I travel? Have you somewhere
left some thing behind that in torment
wants to follow you? Must I go to a country
that without your seeing it was as close
to you as the other half of your senses?

    I will sail its rivers, will
go ashore and ask about old customs,
I will speak to women in doorways
and watch them calling their children.
I will observe how they enter the landscape
out there, by the ancient work of the fields;
I will demand to be led into the presence of their king,
and I will bribe the priests to take me
before the strongest of their statues,
to leave me there, depart, and close the temple gates.
Only then, when I know so much, will I go
simply to observe the animals, so that Something
of their movement slips into my joints;
I want a momentary presence in their eyes
that hold me and release me, slowly,
calmly, without passing judgment.
I will have the gardeners recite
all the flowers for me, so that among the fragments
of their beautiful proper names
I may recover some residue of the hundred fragrances.
And fruits— I will buy fruits, in which
the land is recovered right up to the sky.

    For This you comprehended: the full fruits.

You set them out in bowls before you
and outweighed their heaviness with colors.
You saw the women as fruits too,
and the children molded from inside
into the shapes of their Existence.
And finally you saw yourself as a fruit,
you rid yourself of your clothes, brought
yourself to the mirror, let yourself inside
except for your gaze; huge, it stayed outside,
not saying: that is I; no, but: that is.
So free of curiosity your gaze finally was,
possessing nothing, of so real a poverty,
that it no longer sought even you yourself: holy.

   That's how I want to keep you, as you
put yourself in the mirror, deep inside
and far from everything. Why else do you come?
Why do you deny yourself? Why try to convince me
that in those amber beads around your neck,
something still remains of that heaviness
which the Hereafter of pacified images never has;
why show me so evil a presentiment in your bearing?
Why make me unfold the contours of your body
like the lines of a hand so that I can
no longer see them without including Fate?
   Come here, into the candlelight. I'm not afraid
to look the Dead in the face; when they come,
they have a right to pause in our glance,
like other things.
   Come here; we will be silent a moment.
Look at this rose on my desk;
isn't the light around it just as timid
as that upon you? It too should not be here,
it should have stayed or died outside
in the garden, uninvolved with me,—
see how it survives itself;
what does my knowing mean for the rose?

   Do not fear, if now I comprehend,
when it rises in me: I can do nothing else,

I must comprehend, even if I die of it.
Comprehend, that you are here. I comprehend.
As a blind man comprehends a thing, groping around it,
I feel your Fate and know no name for it.
Let us mourn together, that someone took
you out of your mirror. Can you still weep?
You cannot. You have turned the strength
and pressure of your tears into your full gaze,
and took part in transferring each humor
within you into a strong Existence
that rises and circulates, in equilibrium, blindly.
Then chance tore you, your last chance
tore you back from the limit of your progress,
back into a world where humors *will have their way.*
Did not tear you completely; tore only a shred at first,
yet, when around this shred, from day to day,
Reality expanded, so it grew heavy—
then you needed all of yourself: then you went off
and broke yourself into fragments, out of the law
painstakingly here, because you needed yourself. Then
excavated yourself, and dug out of the soil-bed
of your heart, warm with night, the still-green seeds,
from which your Death should germinate: yours,
your own Death, the one for your own Life.
And ate them, ate the kernels of your Death,
like all the rest, ate its kernels,
and had the aftertaste of sweetness
you did not intend, sweet on your lips,
you: who were already sweet within your senses.

    Let us mourn. Do you know how your blood
hesitantly, reluctantly came back out of
an incomparable orbit, when you recalled it?
How, in confusion, it took up once again
the small circulation of the body; how, full of mistrust
and astonishment, it entered the placenta
and was suddenly exhausted by the long way back.
You drove it on, you thrust it forward,
you dragged it to the hearth, as
a herd of animals is dragged to sacrifice;

and still wanted it to be happy.
And finally you forced it: it was happy
and ran here, and gave itself up. It seemed to you,
because you were used to the other measures,
that it would be only for a while; but
now you were in Time, and Time is long.
It goes by, and goes on,
like a relapse of a long illness.

   How short your life was, compared
to those hours when you sat and silently
bent the various strengths of your various
future to the new Seed-Child
that again was Fate. O difficult task,
a labor beyond all strength! You did it
day after day, you dragged yourself to it
and pulled the beautiful weft from the loom,
using all your threads another way.
And finally still had spirit for celebration.

   Then, because it was completed, you wanted
to be rewarded, like children, after drinking
the bittersweet tea that may restore health.
So you rewarded yourself: because you were, then as now,
still too far from every other; no one could
have conceived of a reward that would please you.
You knew it yourself. You sat up in childbed,
and before you was a mirror, that gave everything
back to you whole. Now everything was *You*
and entirely *outside*, and inside was only deception,
the sweet deception of every woman who gladly
puts on her jewelry and rearranges her hair.

   So you died, as women died before you,
you died in the old way, in the warm house:
the death of women in childbed, who
wanted to close themselves again, but no longer could,
because that darkness, which they also bore,
returns once more, and throngs, and enters.

   Perhaps mourners should have been procured.
Women who weep for money, and if paid well

howl the night through, when it grows still.
Customs! We do not have enough
customs. Everything passes and is abjured.
So, dead, you must come, and here with me
recover mourning. Do you hear me mourn?
I would like to cast my voice like a cloth
over the remnants of your death
and tug at it, until it goes in tatters,
and all that I say would have to
go in rags as well, in this voice, and freeze;
could mourning suffice us. But now I accuse:
not the One, who withdrew you from yourself,
(I do not find him here, he looks like everyone else)
yet in him I accuse everyone else: the man.

   When somewhere having-been-a-child
rises within me, I still don't recognize it,
perhaps the purest childishness of my childhood:
I do not want to know it. I want to form
an angel out of it, without looking at it,
to hurl him into the first rank
of crying angels, that take God in, remembering.

   For this suffering has already lasted too long,
and none can manage it; it is too heavy for us,
the tortuous suffering of false love,
that, building on prescription like a habit,
calls itself justice and prospers on injustice.
Where is a man who has the right to possess?
Who can possess what does not hold itself,
what only from time to time blissfully catches itself
and throws itself again, like a child a ball.
No more than the admiral can hold
a Nike at the prow of his ship,
when the concealed lightness of her godhead
suddenly lifts her into the bright sea-wind:
No more can one of us invoke
the woman who no longer sees us and who
sets forth on the thin strip of her Existence
as through a miracle, without mishap:
then he would have his vocation and pleasure be sin.

For *this* is sin, if anything is sin:
not to widen the freedom of a love
with all the freedom we can summon in ourselves.
We have, where we love, only this:
to release each other; for to hold one another
comes easily to us, and need not be learned.

Are you still there? In which corner are you?—
You have known so much
and were able to do so much, when you departed
open to everything, like a day breaking.
The women suffer: love means being alone,
and artists sometimes surmise in their work
that they must transform where they love.
You began both; both are in That
which now displaces a fame it takes from you.
Oh how far you were from any fame. You were
insignificant; had gently taken in your
beauty, as one furls a flag
on the gray morning of a working day,
and desired nothing but a long work,—
which is not done: for all that, not done.
    If you are still there, if in this darkness
there is still one place in which your spirit
vibrates in time with the shallow sound-waves
that one voice, alone in the night,
calls to a stream in a lofty room:
Hear me: Help me. See, not knowing when,
we slide back, out of our progress
into something we do not intend; in which
we get entangled, as in a dream
and in which we die, without waking.
No one is farther. To each who lifted up
his blood into a work, a long work,
it may happen that he can no longer hold it high
and that it takes its heavy course, worthless.
For somewhere is an old enmity
between the Life and the long Work.
Help me to understand it and to name it.

Do not come back. If you can bear it, be
dead with the dead. The dead are busy.
Yet help me like this, without dispersing yourself,
as the farthest sometimes helps: in me.

Requiem for Wolf Graf von Kalckreuth

[In memoriam W. K., 1887–1906]

Did I never really see you? My heart
is as heavy with you as with a beginning so heavy
that one puts it off. That I might begin to call you
Dead, to tell of you, as you are; you, gladly
passionately Dead. Was it as
disburdening as you supposed, or was
the No-longer-living still far from being dead?
You imagined, better to possess there
where no value is placed on possession. It seemed to you
that there you would be inside the landscape
which always passed before you here as an image,
and from inside you would pass into the beloved
and would proceed through everything, strong and vibrant.
O if only now you would not hold
the deception against your boyish error too long!
If only, dissolved in a stream of sadness
and overcome, only half conscious,
in motion round the distant stars,
you would find the joy you misplaced here,
pushed into the deadness of your dreams.
How close you came to it here, my dear.
How much at home it was, what you meant:
the stern joy of your severe longing.
When disabused by happiness and misfortune
you burrowed into yourself and with one insight
laboriously rose up, almost breaking
under the weight of your dark find:
then you carried it, what you did not recognize,
you carried the joy, the burden of your small savior,
you carried it through your blood and to the other side.
    What you did not prepare for, that the weight
grows unbearable: then it knocks you down
and is so heavy, because it is so real. Do you see,
this was perhaps your next moment:

perhaps it adjusted the garland in its hair
before your door, which you then slammed shut.
    O this blow, how it pierces the universe,
when somewhere from the stiff sharp wind
of impatience, something open is forced to close.
Who can swear that inside the earth
a crack does not run through healthy seeds;
who has inquired whether in tamed animals
a desire to kill does not lewdly, convulsively start
when this shock flashes in their brains?
Who knows the influence of our actions
running over to an immediate peak,
and who follows it there, where everything leads?
    That you have destroyed . . . That this
must be said of you for all time . . .
And when a hero comes, tearing off like a mask
the sense we took for the face of things,
revealing maniacal faces, whose eyes long
and silently gaze at us through dissembling holes:
this is Countenance and will not be transformed:
that you have destroyed. Blocks of stone lay there
and already in the air around them was the rhythm
of a building, no longer to be held back;
one stone concealed the other from you; each one
seemed to take root, when in passing
you tried, without any confidence
you could lift it. And you lifted them all
in despair, but only to hurl them
back into the gaping quarry,
into which, expanded by your heart,
they no longer fit. If only a woman
had rested a gentle hand upon the still fragile
fragile beginning of this rage; if only someone
who was busy, busy at heart,
had met you silently, when you walked out mute
to perform the deed—; yes, if only your path
had led past an awakening workshop,
where men hammer, where the day is realized
simply; if in your full gaze there had been

only space enough for the likeness
of a laboring beetle to enter,
you would have suddenly, in a moment of clarity
read the script whose symbols you had
slowly engraved in yourself since childhood,
from time to time seeing whether a sentence
would form: Oh, it seemed meaningless to you.
I know; I know: you lay before it and wore out
the grooves with too much touching, as we trace
the inscription on a tombstone. Whatever seemed
to burn, you held as a lamp
before the lines; but the flame died
before you understood, perhaps from your breath,
perhaps from your trembling hand; perhaps
entirely by itself, as flames sometimes go out.
You never read it. But we dare not
read through the pain and out of the distance.

We tolerate only the poems that, still
descending the slope of what you've felt,
carry down the words you chose. No,
you did not choose them all; often a beginning
was imposed on you like the whole, a beginning that you repeated
like a command. And it seemed sad to you.
O if only you had never heard it coming from yourself!
Even now your angel speaks the same text, but
with a different accent, and jubilation breaks out
of me hearing how he speaks,
jubilation for you: for this was yours:
That every love would abandon you again,
so that in what you come to see you have
recognized the renunciation, and in death progress.
This was yours, you Artist; these three
open forms. See, here is the outpouring
of the first: space around your feeling; and then
from the second one I tap out for you the gaze
that asks nothing, the gaze of the great artist;
and in the third—which you yourself broke
too soon, when scarcely the first round

of quivering shot from your heart's incandescence
drove in—a death of good work was
deeply molded, one's own death
that needs us so, because we live it,
and which we're never closer to than here.

   All this was your estate and your friendship;
you often surmised it; but then the void
of each form frightened you,
you reached in and scooped out emptiness and
complained.—O ancient curse of poets
who complain where they should speak,
who always pass sentence on their feelings
instead of shaping them; who always take for granted
what is sad or happy in themselves,
this they should know and should be able to praise
or deplore in the poem. Like the sick
they use a woeful language
to describe where it hurts them,
instead of strictly turning themselves into words,
just as the stonemason of a cathedral
transplants himself, obstinately, in the stone's composure.
   This was salvation. If only you had *once*
seen how Fate enters into verses
and does not return, how it becomes image there,
and nothing but image, just as an ancestor
in the frame, when sometimes you look up,
seems to resemble you, and again bears no resemblance—:
you should have held out.

                        But this is petty,
to think of what was not. There is also a semblance
of reproach in the comparison, which does not concern you.
What took place has such a head start
on what we think, on our intentions, that we never catch up
and never come to know how it really looked.
   Don't be ashamed when the dead brush past you,
the other dead, those who held out to
the end. (What does "End" mean?) Exchange

glances with them, calmly, as is the custom,
and don't be afraid our mourning will
burden you so strangely as to attract their attention.
The great words from the times when
event was still visible are not for us.
Who speaks of triumph? Surviving is everything.

Elegy

to Marina Tsvetaeva-Efron

O the losses into the All, Marina, the plunging stars!
We do not augment it, wherever we fling ourselves, toward whatever
star! In Entirety, everything is already counted.
So, whoever falls does not diminish the holy count.
Every relinquishing plunge plunges into the Source and heals.
Would it then all be a game, exchange, displacement,
nowhere a name, and scarcely anywhere familiar gain?
Waves, Marina, we are sea! Depths, Marina, we are heaven!
Earth, Marina, we are earth, we are a thousand times spring, like larks
that a bursting song flings into invisibility.
We begin it as jubilation, already it wholly exceeds us;
suddenly, our weight tips the song down to lament.
What of it: Lament? Wouldn't it be: younger jubilation downward.
Even the lower gods want to be praised, Marina.
So blameless are gods, they await praise like schoolchildren.
Praising, Love, let us be lavish with praise.
Nothing belongs to us. We lay our hand lightly round the throats
of unbroken flowers. I saw it on the Nile, in Kôm-Ombo.
Just so, Marina, the kings, self-renouncing, offer bounty.
Just as the angels walk and mark the doors of those to be saved,
we, who seem to be tender, touch upon this and that.
Oh, as if far away already, oh, as if scattered,
even in our inmost pretext! Signallers, nothing more.
This gentle commerce, when one of our kind
no longer endures it and resolves to seize,
avenges itself and kills. For its power to kill
was plain to us all in its restraint and its delicacy
and by its strange power that turns us from living beings
into survivors. Not-being. Do you know how often
a blind command carried us through the icy anteroom
of new birth. . . . Carried: *us?* body of eyes
under countless lids, refusing. Carried the downfallen
heart in us, the heart of an entire race. To a goal of migrant birds
it carried the flock, the image of our hovering transformation.
Lovers ought not, Marina, may not

know so much of decline. Must be as new.
Only their grave is old, only their grave remembers, darkens
under the sobbing tree, remembers Everness.
Only their grave breaks open; they themselves are supple as reeds;
what bends them too far rounds them richly to the garland.
How they are blown about in the May-wind! The Moment bars them
from the center of Ever, in which you breathe and surmise.
(O how I understand you, female blossom on the same
immutable shrub. How richly I spread myself into the night breeze,
that will strip you soon.) The gods were quick to learn how
to simulate halves. We, drawn into the circle,
filled ourselves out to the Whole like the moon's disc.
Even in waning phases, even in the weeks of turning
no one would ever help us again to Fullness, except for our own
solitary course over the sleepless landscape.

Antistrophes

Oh that here, women, you pace, stately
here among us, sorrowful,
no more sheltered than we and still able
to bless like the blessed.

From what place,
when the beloved appears,
do you secure the future?
More than ever will be.
One who knows the distances
even up to the farthest fixed star,
is astonished when he discovers
the sovereign space of your heart.
How, in the crowd, do you spare it?
You, full of sources and night.

Are you really the same ones
who were children
on the way to school
brusquely cuffed by the older brother?
You whole ones.

Where we as children already
hideously disfigured ourselves forever,
you were like bread before the Change.

Breaking with childhood
did you no harm. All at once
you stood there, as if in God
suddenly completing the miracle.

We, as if broken off from the mountain,
even as boys, sharp
at the edges, or
sometimes nicely hewn;
we, like fragments of rock
dumped over flowers.

Flowers of the deeper earth,
beloved of all roots,
you, sisters of Eurydice,
always full of holy return
behind the ascending man.

　　We, self-afflicted,
　　gladly afflicting, gladly
　　afflicted once again out of need.
　　We, like weapons at anger's disposal
　　laid down beside sleep.

You, who are almost protection, where no one
protects. For the swarms of the solitary
the thought of you is like
a shading Tree of Sleep.

The Sonnets to Orpheus II, 13

Come before all departure, as if it were behind you,
like the winter, that passes even now. For among
winters, beneath them, there is one so endless, that
your heart, wintering, passing through that winter,
without counting days, really does survive, transcends.

Be ever dead in Eurydice—, let the songs come,
rise, praising, praising rise, back into the pure relation,
the store. Here, among the Dwindling, be,
in the Realm of Decline, be a ringing glass
that already in sounding shattered to nothing.

Be— and know at the same time Not-Being,
the unending ground of your inmost vibration,
so that you accomplish it this
one time.

To the consumed, as well as to the muffled, damp and dumb
storehouse of full Nature, the unspeakable, the immense sums,
add yourself, count yourself among them, jubilantly, and
cancel the count.

Pearls rolling away! Oh, did a string break?
But what good would it do to string them again? I need you,
strong clasp that restrained them, beloved.

Wasn't it time? As dawn the sunrise,
I wait to confront you, pale from the night completed;
like a full theater, I form one huge face,
so that nothing of your noble central
appearance escapes me. O as a gulf hopes into open
seas, and from its outstretched lighthouse
casts shining spaces; like a riverbed of the desert,
waiting for the rain of the pure mountains to ravish it, the rain still
    of the sky,—
like the prisoner who stands at his blameless window
longing for the answer of the one star;
like a cripple who throws away
the warm crutches, so that someone may hang them up, there,
on the altar, and lies down there, and without a miracle cannot rise:
see, if you do not come, just like that I will stumble to my end.

I desire only you. The crack in the pavement
when it, wretchedly, wants to grow grass: must it not desire
the entire spring? Look— the spring of the earth.
Does not the moon, to find itself, to find its image in the village pond,
need the great illumination of the strange star? How can
the most trivial thing occur, if the fullness of the future,
if every moment of counted time, does not move toward us?

Are you not finally in it, Inexpressible? Just a while longer,
and I will endure you no more. I grow old or I am
pushed aside by children . . .

The Sonnets to Orpheus II, 29

Still friend of the many distances, feel
how your breath, your breathing still enlarges Space.
Among the beams of the dark bell towers,
let yourself sound, resound. What feeds on you,
what consumes and wastes you, in feeding

becomes a Strength beyond that nourishment.
Give yourself to Transformation: Know its house.
Even if you yourself are consumed.
What experience made you suffer most?
If drinking is bitter to you, become the wine.

In this immeasurable night, this Night of
Excess, be that magic power at the crossroads
of your Senses. Be Sense, the significance
of their strange, their special meeting.

And if the Earthly has forgotten you,
say to the still and silent earth: I flow.
To the hasty water say:
                              I am.

(To a friend of Wera's)

Come, you last thing I recognize,
unendurable pain in the body's web:
Just as I burned in spirit, see, I burn
in you; the wood has long resisted
joining its voice to your flame;
but now I feed you and burn in you.
My gentleness of earth, in your rage,
becomes a rage of Hell, not of here.
Planless, wholly pure, free of future,
I mounted pain's tortuous pyre,
sure of never buying a Becoming
with this heart, where all resource was mute.
Am I still unrecognizable; what burns?
I shall not drag memories inside.
O living, Living: To be outside.
And I in flames. No one who knows me.

(Renunciation. This is not what sickness once was
in childhood. Postponement. Pretext for
growing. Everything called, admonishing.
Do not confuse this with what amazed you long ago.)

The Lockert Library of Poetry in Translation

George Seferis: Collected Poems (1924–1955), translated, edited, and introduced by Edmund Keeley and Philip Sherrard

Collected Poems of Lucio Piccolo, translated and edited by Brian Swann and Ruth Feldman

C. P. Cavafy: Collected Poems, translated by Edmund Keeley and Philip Sherrard and edited by George Savidis

Benny Andersen: Selected Poems, translated by Alexander Taylor

Selected Poetry of Andrea Zanzotto, translated and edited by Ruth Feldman and Brian Swann

Poems of René Char, translated by Mary Ann Caws and Jonathan Griffin

Selected Poems of Tudor Arghezi, translated and edited by Michael Impey and Brian Swann

"The Survivor" and Other Poems by Tadeusz Różewicz, translated and introduced by Magnus J. Krynski and Robert A. Maguire

"Harsh World" and Other Poems by Ángel González, translated by Donald D. Walsh

Ritsos in Parentheses, translations and introduction by Edmund Keeley

Salamander: Selected Poems of Robert Marteau, translated by Anne Winters

Angelos Sikelianos: Selected Poems, translated and introduced by Edmund Keeley and Philip Sherrard

Dante's "Rime," translated by Patrick S. Diehl

Selected Later Poems of Marie Luise Kaschnitz, translated by Lisel Mueller

Osip Mandelstam's "Stone," translated and introduced by Robert Tracy

The Dawn Is Always New: Selected Poetry of Rocco Scotellaro, translated by Ruth Feldman and Brian Swann

Sounds, Feelings, Thoughts: Seventy Poems by Wisława Szymborska, translated and introduced by Magnus J. Krynski and Robert A. Maguire

The Man I Pretend to Be: "The Colloquies" and Selected Poems of Guido Gozzano, translated and edited by Michael Palma, with an introductory essay by Eugenio Montale

D'Après Tout: Poems by Jean Follain, translated by Heather McHugh

Songs of Something Else: Selected Poems of Gunnar Ekelöf, translated by Leonard Nathan and James Larson

The Little Treasury of One Hundred People, One Poem Each, compiled by Fujiwara No Sadaie and translated by Tom Galt

The Ellipse: Selected Poems of Leonardo Sinisgalli, translated by W. S. Di Piero

The Difficult Days by Roberto Sosa, translated by Jim Lindsey

Hymns and Fragments by Friedrich Hölderlin, translated and introduced by Richard Sieburth

Rilke: Between Roots. Selected poems rendered from the German by Rika Lesser

LIBRARY OF CONGRESS CATALOGING-IN-PUBLICATION DATA

Rilke, Rainer Maria, 1875-1926.
  Rilke: between roots.
  (The Lockert library of poetry in translation)
  Rev. ed. of: Holding out. c1975.
   1. Rilke, Rainer Maria, 1875-1926—Translations, English. I. Lesser, Rika. II.
Rilke, Rainer Maria, 1875-1926. Holding out. III. Title. IV. Series.
PT2635.I65A2522   1986   831'.912   85-43204
ISBN 0-691-01429-9 (pbk.)   ISBN 0-691-06668-X (alk. paper)